It's Not All About "Me":

The Top Ten Techniques for Building Quick Rapport
with Anyone

By: Robin K. Dreeke

It's Not All About "Me": The Top Ten Techniques for Building Quick Rapport with Anyone Copyright © 2011 Robin K. Dreeke

Editing by: Cynthia Lewis; Chris Hadnagy.

Cover Photo: © Sergey Ilin, Dreamstime.com

The views expressed in this work are solely those of the author and not those of the FBI.
For more information please visit www.peopleformula.com

To my beautiful wife and wonderful children; without your support, encouragement, and example this book would not have been possible. To all my friends and family my heartfelt thanks for continually showing me the way. To my great friends Cynthia and Chris, thanks for your endurance, tenacity and never ending selfless help.

Man in the Arena

"It is not the critic who counts: not the man who points out how the strong man stumbles or where the doer of deeds could have done better. The credit belongs to the man who is actually in the arena, whose face is marred by dust and sweat and blood, who strives valiantly, who errs and comes up short again and again, because there is no effort without error or shortcoming, but who knows the great enthusiasms, the great devotions, who spends himself for a worthy cause; who, at the best, knows, in the end, the triumph of high achievement, and who, at the worst, if he fails, at least he fails while daring greatly, so that his place shall never be with those cold and timid souls who knew neither victory nor defeat."

Theodore Roosevelt "Citizenship in a Republic,"
Speech at the Sorbonne, Paris, April 23, 1910

Table of Contents

Introduction 7

Identifying the Need 10

Technique 1: Establishing Artificial Time Constraints 13

Technique 2: Accommodating Nonverbals 19

Technique 3: Slower Rate of Speech... 28

Technique 4: Sympathy or Assistance Theme................................... 33

Technique 5: Ego Suspension... 41

Technique 6: Validate Others 49

    Validation Technique 1: Listening 49

    Validation Technique 2: Thoughtfulness...................................... 52

    Validation Technique 3: Validate Thoughts and Opinions 54

Technique 7: Ask... How? When? Why? 57

Technique 8: Connect With Quid Pro Quo.. 66

Technique 9: Gift Giving (Reciprocal Altruism)............................... 72

Technique 10: Manage Expectations... 77

Putting it all together: 83

Practice Exercises:.. 86

    Exercise 1: Third Party Reference.. 87

    Exercise 2: Artificial Time Constraints 89

    Exercise 3: Slower Rate of Speech... 91

Exercise 4: Sympathy or Assistance Theme 92

Exercise 5: Ego Suspension 94

Exercise Summary: 96

Bibliography... 97

Introduction

What if I told you there was a way to gain the skills of master communicators? Skills that can enable you to induce any stranger to divulge inner-most secrets, banking information, or even take actions against your best interests, all voluntarily? These people don't have any different ability or skills than you have or use every day. The difference is they know what these ten techniques are and how to employ them effectively and consciously.

This book is unique because it contains a very actionable process for how to treat individuals exactly how we all wish we were treated every minute of every day of our lives. This book is also different because this process of how to truly focus on others is written from my point of view and my experiences as a former Marine Corps officer, FBI special agent and program manager of the FBI's elite Behavioral Analysis Program. The leadership and interpersonal skills I needed to develop as a Marine Corps officer and an FBI agent are capsulated in this workbook formatted guide.

I am going to share what I have found is the most successful way to face all aspects of life, both personal and professional. This process has been honed from years of field experience, as well as research into social and evolutionary psychology. The results from the process will range from simply making those around you truly enjoy your company and seek to spend more time with you all the way up to influencing others to take actions you want them to take. Regardless of your individual goals, the key is to make it "all about them."

Studies have demonstrated time after time that the happiest individuals in the world are the ones with meaningful relationships. Those who have both a wide array of friends and acquaintances as well as relationships of deep meaning with a few acquaintances tend to be happier in life than those who have placed items and material accomplishments as their individual goals for happiness. These ten simple steps, whether used completely or in parts will have a profoundly positive impact on the quality of any relationship in your life, whether the relationship is at home, work, play, or simply talking with strangers.

As technology has moved forward and brought the world closer together through social networking sites like Facebook, Twitter, and numerous other online social sites, many of the one on-one skills utilized to develop rapport and deeper relationships is falling prey to the ease and convenience of just turning off a computer when something isn't said just right or one of your hundreds of contacts / friends on Facebook says something that annoys you. The easy fix is to just pay attention to one of the other of hundreds of people you are in contact with on a daily basis in one way or another. One of the critical elements missing from this wonderful technology that has brought individuals from all over the world together is the ability to have meaningful one-on-one conversation.

The art of conversation and developing rapport with an individual, whether a friend, loved one, work associate, or stranger, comes down to the ability of at least one of the individuals dialoging to do at least one of the ten concepts I am going to illustrate in this book. As you read each section that highlights one of the ten techniques, think back to a good conversation or relationship that you have had throughout your life. I will bet that if the conversation was enjoyable to you, whether you were speaking to a friend or stranger, at least one of the ten elements was present. A conversation that has two to four of the elements will be one you will remember for a very long time. A conversation that has nine to ten of the elements will be remembered for a lifetime.

Identifying the Need

I will start our journey through this process by first stating that I discovered how to identify these steps because I desperately needed it. Discovering these tools and techniques was and continues to be a great challenge and adventure. I have found that I generally say I'm sorry more than most people I know. I think this is true because I sometimes stray from my own process, as well as I am highly aware of myself and the impact I have on others through nonverbal observations. Unlike the great many wonderful people in my life, I was not designed by either my biology or any higher power to be as strongly people oriented as others. Studies of personality assessments such as the Myers Briggs Type Indicator (MBTI), the Five Factor Model, the Personality Discernment Instrument (DISC), and many others identify that about 50% of the population tends to be people oriented. These are the types of individuals who ask you about your day and family, wait to hear the answer, and truly care about the answer. The other 50% of us roll through life generally a bit more self-absorbed and unwitting to the emotional damage we cause by our insensitive comments, our self-centered conversations, or our inability for empathy or personalization.

Regardless of the fact that I care very deeply for many people and feel great compassion and empathy, at times, my ability to accurately communicate those feelings has fallen short of the mark. For many individuals such as myself, the fact that the way you feel about a situation or person can look, sound, and feel very incongruent with those you are communicating with. This book will help people naturally communicating effectively as well as those who want to improve their ability to make good connections, communicate effectively, and even influence individuals if they so desire.

My first awareness of needing to improve my skills and realizing it is not all about "me" occurred while I was a midshipman at the U.S. Naval Academy. I am a very outgoing person who enjoys meeting strangers and having lively discussions on just about any topic. I find people fascinating and intriguing and really enjoy getting to know them. Unfortunately, when I was 18 years old I also had a very bad habit of being judgmental of others. Having a "big mouth" and voicing my opinions openly didn't help matters. I had a great deal of self-confidence and thought that if the whole world were just a bit more like me it would be perfect and we would all get along wonderfully. I also felt compelled for some reason to voice my dissent of those who didn't fit into my perception of the perfect world.

During my four years at the Naval Academy and my five on active duty as a Marine Corps officer, I was slowly learning that I was inadvertently causing hurt feelings, discomfort, and negative thoughts about me because of my insensitive words and actions. Each time this happened, I was shocked and embarrassed. I was realizing that, often, the way I was communicating my thoughts and ideas was not accurate portrayals of how I truly felt inside. Have you ever had this situation? If so, then you will benefit from this book.

As I matured and became more self-aware, these instances were fewer and the severity of the effect I sometimes had was less, but they still did occur. Causing ill feelings and discomfort bothered me greatly. The combination of becoming a husband and father aided the process of self-regulation, but not until I became an FBI agent and eventually both an instructor and in charge of the Behavioral Analysis Program was I able to take all the skills I had learned in the field as a successful street agent into actionable tools. When I began developing my own self-awareness of the process, I was truly amazed, and hopefully you will be, at how translatable these skills are into every aspect of our lives. As a matter of fact, I have found that I have more examples of these tools in action when dialoging with my family, neighbors, and even strangers in a checkout line than I do as an FBI special agent. This is because all of us are human beings and respond to the same biological and personal needs and wants in any situation. My deepest desire is that you will find this book usable in the many complex aspects of your life and that you are able to build stronger relationships with those you know, make strangers feel better about themselves, and, ultimately, feel great about the type of person you are. Research has shown that the happiest individuals in the world are those with strong interpersonal relationships, regardless of any material wealth they do or do not have.

Technique 1: Establishing Artificial Time Constraints

Have you ever been sitting in a bar, an airport, a library, or browsing in a bookstore when a stranger tried to start a conversation with you? Did you feel awkward or on your guard? The conversation itself is not necessarily what caused the discomfort. The discomfort was induced because you didn't know when or if it would end. For this reason, the first step in the process of developing great rapport and having great conversations is letting the other person know that there is an end in sight, and it is really close.

I recently was giving a class on advanced approach techniques. In this class we go over each of these techniques in great detail and then practice them live in whatever area of the country we may be. This particular class was the first one I had developed where the students would have to go out in the middle of the afternoon during lunch-time and approach individuals using the techniques we are discussing here. The only objective was to have a meaningful conversation with someone and learn their full name and a bit more about them than what they were having for lunch. To be successful, they had to get a little more personal.

When I teach my classes, I also participate in the same tasks as the attendees. I do this because it ensures I am fully aware of the types of venues that the class is operating in and it keeps my skills sharp and ever enhancing as well. During this particular exercise, I had chosen an area that had a busy Panera Bread Company. Compounding the high tempo of the area was the fact that it was 1pm on a busy lunch hour. My plan was to practice at this venue, and I noticed that a few of my students had followed me in. Now I really felt the pressure.

This was a difficult environment to have a deep conversation with a stranger anyway. The place was packed with a line out the door, had very little sitting room, and now I was being watched by my students. I needed to be on my "A" game.

Regardless of being watched or not, the most important thing to have is confidence in the process. The process and the techniques are specifically designed around our human genetics and biology to maximize our potential success. When you have confidence in the process and techniques, you also will look calmer and not look, as my daughter says, "awkward."

I was standing in the long line waiting to order a salad. was scanning the area for a conversation opportunity. While scanning, I went through my plan and techniques to ensure I wa ready when a situation presented itself. I believe in using conversational nonthreatening "themes" in my dialogues. M themes are also based around my life and what is currently going on in it. Again, when you are discussing things that have meaning and are truthful, it is much easier to make a positive connection. I do not believe in lying when engaging individuals However, I may exaggerate from time to time about how much may enjoy a particular hobby or interest, but I will never deceive about my knowledge and/or experience of the same; it is to easy to spot insincerity.

The theme that had come up recently in my house was dating age. My daughter at the time was 13 years old and w were having some good discussions about what an appropria

14

dating age is. [email me sometime and I'll give you my thoughts] I had used this theme a few times already with really fun and exciting results. One evening I had gone with a class to a local restaurant and sat at the busy bar. I initiated the question about dating age to the bartender and within 15 minutes the entire bar area was engaged in the conversation with many topical offshoots.

Back at the Panera restaurant, the clerk behind the counter finally called my number. I maneuvered my way through the sea of people to pick up my order. I took my salad and began the slow walk while scanning for a seat. Out of the corner of my eye, I noticed some of my students watching me with a grin that implied, "Ok, let's see how you deal with this place." I gave them a slight nod as I tried to hide my anxiety of potentially failing in front of them when, to my relief, I found a small two-person table in the sea of tables and bodies. Before I sat down, I quickly noted a gentleman that looked to be a "baby boomer" (an individual typically born between the years of 1945-1965.) Part of the exercise this day was to approach an individual from a different generation.

The gentleman was dressed nicely in a business casual button up shirt and dress pants. His hair was graying and combed neatly to the back and side. He was eating a sandwich and entirely engrossed in reading material on his smartphone. His two-person table was to the left of mine, and I sat down so that we were facing each other.

I sat there and began eating my salad and strategized how I was going to initiate and have a productive conversation with someone clearly engaged with and completely content reading on his smartphone. I thought that because his chair was facing

15

mine, he might glance up at some point, and I could engage then. To my dismay, as my salad was disappearing, he never once lifted his head.

Trusting in the techniques and methods, I decided to use what I call "implied artificial time constraints." I knew that the man was not regarding me but probably picked me up in his peripheral vision. I also figured that once I initiated a dialogue, he would quickly assess the situation to determine whether it was threatening or not. Most human beings assess new situations and people for threat before anything else. Humans have genetically survived because of this. This is a strong reason why these techniques work; they are specifically designed to lower the perceived risk to a stranger.

The implied artificial time constraint I decided to use was my salad. I also decided to take out my own smartphone and begin to peruse e-mail in a nonverbal matching gesture. Nonverbal matching can be used effectively if done lightly and in non-obvious ways. In this particular case I planned on using the prop of my smartphone to aid in the initiation of the conversation.

I finally finished my salad and put both my napkin and fork on the plate and pushed it away to the other side of the table, implying that I was done and getting ready to leave. This action was the implied time constraint. I regarded my smartphone again while facing the gentleman and frowned while furrowing my brow. I then leaned in toward the gentleman so he could hear me and said, "I'm sorry to bother you. I'm about to leave and have been having a tough conversation with my wife (I implied nonverbally that it was through the blackberry email. I have a teenage daughter, and she is on social networking site and the like. What do you think is an appropriate age for girls to start dating?" (I threw out the social networking sites as well, even though it wasn't relative to the primary question. That was to add one more content topic in case he wanted to discuss that topic, too.)

As I was asking my question and establishing my stated artificial time constraints, "I'm about to leave," I noted the man assessing the situation for threat. He first looked at me with a puzzled look and facial compression. (Compression can indicate stress.) He next looked at the smartphone in my hand and my finished salad on the table. All of my surroundings were congruent with the words being spoken. Both the congruence of events and statements, as well as the artificial time constraints, must have satisfied the gentleman. He smiled broadly and stated, "I have a 25 and a 23 year old daughter." I replied, "Ahh, I have an expert." He laughed and began talking about his thoughts, opinions, and ideas.

As the rest of the techniques unfold throughout this book, I will use this and other stories to illustrate how each technique was used to elicit a wonderful conversation from anyone of our choosing. In this case, the gentleman spoke with me for almost thirty minutes about his daughters, their first boyfriends and how he and his wife have handled the "empty nest" syndrome with them moving out. I had originally stated and then nonverbally implied I was leaving right then. By establishing those artificial time constraints, the gentleman's perception of a threat was lowered, and he readily engaged for a much longer time. As a matter of fact, at one point I got up to leave. As I thanked him, he started on another conversation and I sat back down and continued to listen.

It is very important to remember that not one technique can guarantee success. Even perfect execution of all techniques cannot guarantee success. The proper execution of as many techniques as possible will greatly enhance your probability of success and ensure you will have better conversations and more meaningful rapport than you would have otherwise.

There are experiential exercises at the end of the book for you to try. The purpose of the exercises are to illustrate that these techniques don't just sound good on paper but that you can be very successful executing them yourself. I have not had an individual in any of my seminars yet say that they didn't believe in the process and techniques once they tried them for themselves. You can try the exercises as you read or wait until the end. I would offer that the more you practice, the better you will become.

There are not many places that teach these advanced techniques. By the end of this book and related exercises, you will have experienced your own self-education in this area, as well as demonstrated multiple successes with each technique. The exercises are not meant to be either hard or time-consuming. The key to remember when practicing each of the techniques is that each builds upon the last and that not all the individuals you will be chatting with are ready to receive the gift you are about to give them... the gift of a great conversation with you. Each person you engage should walk away at the end feeling great about themselves and the conversation with you.

Technique 2: Accommodating Nonverbals

Did you ever see a photograph of someone and say, "He looks like a pompous idiot." The opening statement and actions in any interaction set the tone for the engagement, as well as establish whether the individual being engaged will look upon you favorably or unfavorably. In the last chapter we discussed artificial time constraints. Next on the list of techniques is accommodating nonverbals. This chapter will explore how to "look" like a nonthreatening nice person to converse with.

Most of us are already good at recognizing nonverbal demeanor. We don't necessarily register it consciously, but once given a few labels like we are about to do, we can be much more proactive in our nonverbal assessments. For example, ask yourself if you know when someone at work is having a bad day. You probably recognize when someone is having a bad day, even without them saying a word. This is because they "look different." That is to say, they look different from what they normally look like on every other day.

When you walk into a room with a bunch of strangers, are you naturally drawn to those who look angry and upset or those with smiles and laughing? Smiling is the number one nonverbal technique you should utilize to look more accommodating. In Dale Carnegie's book, "How to Win Friends and Influence People" it is principle number two of six. In my many years of leadership in the government, as well as in the development of confidential human sources, I have found that a genuine smile goes a long way in developing rapport.

Smiling is a great baseline behavior to exhibit in order to establish rapport, but it can be accentuated through the subtle use of a few other nonverbal head displays. Adding a slight head tilt shows the other person that you have comfort with them and trust them. Another nonverbal to try and maintain is a slightly lower chin angle. High chin angles give the impression of looking down your nose at someone and that you are aloof or better than them. The following photos give some great examples of accommodating nonverbal head displays.

Practice exercise:

The best way to get good and natural at displaying accommodating nonverbal of the face and head is to practice. First, look into a mirror and regard your "normal" look. Once you have established your normal look, simply say out loud, "Hi, how are you?" Next, give yourself a slight head tilt, ensure your head is very slightly angled down as shown above and smile as you say again, "Hi, how are you?" You should both look and feel differently when attempting this very simple yet effective exercise.

This technique requires a great deal of practice if you do not naturally have accommodating nonverbals. We all have some from time to time, but, in situations when it matters most, it is good to have experience with displaying the best you can. Displaying accommodating nonverbal behavior is not difficult or complex. Like many of the other techniques, these alone may not work. But in conjunction with the other techniques, you will most likely have more engaging conversations with friends and strangers.

Every individual is different, and I have found for myself that working from the top of the body down is the easiest way to practice and check myself. Working from the top down is generally more effective because individuals tend to focus on the head and face. Accommodating facial nonverbals will go a long way to building quick rapport. I recently had an incident with someone who was clearly in a fit of road rage toward me. I consciously lowered my chin, tilted my head, and utilized a subdued friendly smile while apologizing. Imagine how the conversation would have gone had I apologized with my head tilted back with a smirk on my face? Mr. Road Rage would read my face as not being genuine in my apology and would have escalated the conflict even more.

Another favorite accommodating nonverbal I like to use is body angle. Especially when meeting someone for the first time it is important to have a nonthreatening body angle. When two people stand toe to toe, it can be very intimidating, especially if they are strangers. A slight body angle or blade away from the individual you are engaging will present a much more accommodating nonverbal.

Notice how Vice President Biden is standing with no body angle toward Sarah Palin. Sarah Palin on the other hand is bladed at an angle and even leaning back a little. Vice President

Biden was not demonstrating accommodating nonverbals and Sarah Palin is reacting negatively to him.

A great example of the power of accommodating nonverbals happened when I was on a trip with a colleague out in San Francisco. I was making a presentation on Social Engineering and how to elicit information to a group of law enforcement executives. Following the conference, my colleague and I were sitting in the hotel's lobby. The lobby was spacious and had a coffee counter that served coffee, dessert pastries, etc. A young woman walked up to the counter to order a coffee. My friend and I were sitting sipping on our own coffee about 30 feet away and my friend noticed that the woman was wearing knee-high boots. My friend explained that he was in the market for a pair of boots like that as a gift for his wife. He went on to ask me if I wouldn't mind using a little subterfuge to get a photo of the boots so he could show his wife to check whether she liked the style. My friend went on to explain this elaborate scheme of pretending to photograph him with my cell phone with her innocently in the background. I looked at him doubtfully and said, "I'll just go ask her."

I quickly put my plan in place using the ten techniques. The main objective in all engagements is simple; the person you are engaging must leave the conversation and interaction feeling better for having met you. This primary goal will help ensure success. I always want to ensure that I do not give the impression that I have romantic interests in any target, male or female. For that reason, I always rely upon a theme that I am trying to do something very special for my wife. I also strongly believe in sticking to the truth; if you are ever caught in a lie or deception, the relationship is damaged greatly. In this specific encounter, I

23

had to ensure I used accommodating nonverbals, as well as established artificial time constraints.

The young lady was standing at the counter awaiting her beverage when I approached. I bladed my body to not face her directly. I then ensured that my head angle was slightly down and that I had a pleasant smile with a slight head tilt. I said, "Hi, my friend and I have to leave in a second, and I am very sorry to bother you, but I was hoping you could help me." The young lady didn't back away but had a quizzical look on her face as she sheepishly said, "ok…." I quickly explained that my friend was searching for the perfect gift for his wife for a special anniversary they had coming up. The young lady began relaxing a bit more as her beverage was delivered from the barista. I explained how my friend was looking for a pair of boots like the ones that she was wearing but wasn't sure if his wife would like them. The young lady quickly interrupted explaining how she came to purchase the boots herself from a store down the block. She went on to describe how much they cost and what she liked and didn't like about them. I validated each of her statements and continued to encourage her to talk about a topic that she apparently enjoyed. When she was finished with her description of the boots, I asked if she wouldn't mind if I took a picture of the boots so that my friend could check with his wife if these were the type of boots that she would like. The young lady was very happy to accommodate and posed for multiple photos.

During the dialogue, I also was able to obtain a vast amount of personal information about where the young lady worked, grew up, her full name, family background, and other details. The entire exchange took 12 minutes. As the young lady departed, I thanked her for her time and offered to buy her another coffee. She declined and thanked me for such a good chat.

The story is a great example of how powerful each technique can be. Using the techniques is very similar to giving a gift. A gift in general terms is an action taken and given when thinking solely of another individual's needs and wants. When using these techniques, each of us is ultimately thinking solely about the other person. In other words, it is not about me.

The final accommodating nonverbal that is easy to incorporate into your behavior is the handshake. An accommodating handshake is one that matches the strength of the other, and also takes more of a palm up angle. Note again the photo of Vice President Biden and Sarah Palin. Her hand is palm up and his is palm down in a dominance display. Sarah Palin was not necessarily trying to be accommodating in this situation, but her nonverbals were. Likewise, Vice President Biden was clearly not demonstrating accommodating nonverbals.

A few years ago I also noted former presidential candidate Mike Huckabee in a media photo. He was doing the same thing. Mike Huckabee demonstrates excellent accommodating nonverbal behavior. He generally has a lower chin angle; he leans in to listen with a slight head tilt and shakes hands palm up. Some have said that this may be because of his days as a pastor greeting individuals following a service. Whichever the case is, he is another great example of accommodating nonverbal.

All of the ten techniques alone will not guarante
success. Please remember that not everyone is ready to receiv
the gift you are offering. These techniques will greatly enhanc
your chances of a successful conversation and engagement, bu
some people may be in an emotional place at the time of th

engagement where they are not willing to receive these special gifts and accommodating nonverbals. Do not take it personally; remember, it is not that they are doing it to you, it is all about them.

Technique 3: Slower Rate of Speech

The last chapter discussed how to "look" more accommodating by ensuring we have accommodating and open nonverbal body language. The next technique is also considered "nonverbal" even though it is about speaking. There are many aspects to our voice that are nonverbal. Nonverbals of the voice merely refer to the tempo, modulation, and inclination of your voice, to name a few. When individuals speak slowly and clearly, they tend to sound more credible than those who speak quickly.

Our natural rate of speech is going to depend on many factors besides our individual genetics and biology. For the purpose of this guide, we will explore two that we can consciously adjust if we choose to. The first is to what degree an individual is extroverted. According to the Meyers Briggs Type Indicator based upon the work of psychologist Carl Jung individuals who are extroverted derive their energy from the external world. As an extroverted individual converses with other people, the energy level of the individual increases. The increased energy level often-times will manifest itself in a higher rate of speech. Approximately 50% of the population has a preference for extroversion.

The preference for extroversion does not mean that we are limited in how each of us can interact with the world. Like many of our traits and qualities, this is merely the starting point. Preferences for how we prefer to engage other people are just that, preferences.

Preference Exercise: For example, take out a piece of paper and a pen or pencil. Sign your name twice.

Next: Switch hands with the pen or pencil and sign your name again twice.

On the same piece of paper list a few words that describe how it felt when you signed your name with your dominant or "preferred hand." Some of the more common adjectives I have heard are:

1. Easy
2. Fast
3. I didn't have to think about it
4. No problem

Make another list for what you thought and felt regarding signing with your non-dominant or non-preferred hand. This list typically includes adjectives such as:

1. Geez
2. Tough
3. I had to think about it
4. I had to write much slower
5. I think I may have a problem
6. My two-year-old son writes better

These responses are typical. We all have a genetic preference for which hand we prefer to write with. Think for a minute if you ever lost use of your dominant hand. I often have individuals in my classes who have had their dominant hand incapacitated for a period of time. Over time they develop the ability to write and function much easier with their non-dominant hand. They chose out of necessity to become better at their non-biological preferred hand.

I love this illustration because it demonstrates one of my critical concepts that I subscribe to. I do not believe in trying to "change" people. When someone says, "You need to change." Or, "I can change her." I think you are setting yourself up for a disappointing task. Many psychologists subscribe to the theory that much of our personalities are based upon genetics and biology. Personalities are deeply impacted by our individual experiences that shape them, but ultimately we are born with our personality fundamentals. We cannot change our biology or genetics, but we can enhance or dampen them when needed and when we choose to.

When required, each of us would be able to choose to get better at writing with our non-dominant hand. Likewise, when called upon, each of us can modify our rate of speech when we choose to. The power of modifying ourselves isn't limited to rate of speech. It can also be applied to every step in this process. Having tools empowers us with choice about how to interact with the world around us.

The other major factor that can define our rate of speech is our demographics, or where we grew up in the country or world. Demographics have a significant impact on not just rate of speech but in many other ways that each of us views the world around us. For example, I grew up in lower New York State, not too far north of New York City. Where I grew up, the vast majority of individuals who enjoyed following sports were avid professional sports fans. I happen to be a New York Yankee and New York Jets fan. All the media outlets in New York cover professional sports at a very deep level. A number of years ago when my wife and I moved to Virginia, I was astounded by the difference regarding sports. The majority of sports fans I have met and who are my friends and colleagues in this region are avid college sports fans. On Saturdays during college football season, most houses in our subdivision can be seen flying the flag of either University of Virginia or Virginia Tech. I am always fascinated by the differences for each of our preferences based upon demographics.

Whereas our rate of speech is impacted largely by our biology and genetics, like in the sports analogy, it is impacted by our demographics. Some individuals like me who grew up in New York or even New England are thought to be more of "quick talkers." Just like in the handwriting example, I can choose to alter my preference for the speed with which I speak. This need became apparent to me one day when working in my unit at FBI headquarters a few years ago.

One day, a few of my fellow agents and I were standing outside our cubicles discussing an urgent matter concerning an operational scenario for an investigation that one of the special agents in "the field" was trying to conduct. Each of us had an opinion and most were looking to me and what I had to say about it because of my experience and background in the area. I had conducted the type of operation numerous times before and became very animated and excited because I was so familiar with the content. My confidence in the topic, my extroversion and my New York demographics enabled me to unwittingly increase my speech tempo dramatically. Toward the end of the discussion, I clearly remember one of my friends leaning over to me as we were standing in the conversation circle and quietly saying, "We all know how credible you are Robin. When you

31

speak that fast you lose your credibility. Slow it down so you are not overselling, and stop appearing as though you are trying to sell us a bad used car."

The realization of my friend's observation made a very profound and positive impact on me. From that day forward, I began to notice my speech tempo. Whenever I have a conversation that I believe is important for me to be credible in my content, I purposely slow down the delivery and take pauses for people to absorb the content of what I have just said.

This translates to meeting and chatting with strangers very easily. Speak slower when having a dialogue and you will not come across as the "bad used car salesman." This was illustrated very well in the story I told in chapter 2 about how was able to take photographs of the young woman's boots at the coffee house in San Francisco. I used all the techniques we are discussing here, and I delivered them with a slow rate of speech. Like all the techniques, just using one will not guarantee success but the compounded effect of as many as you can do will greatly enhance your odds of a great conversation and better rapport and relationships.

Technique 4: Sympathy or Assistance Theme

Have you ever felt a pang of guilt for turning down someone seeking help? I have personally found that there is no greater theme and tool for eliciting individuals for action, information, and a great conversation than the use of sympathy or assistance. Think for a moment about the times in your life when you have either sought assistance or been asked to provide it. When the request is simple, of limited duration, and non-threatening, we are more inclined to accommodate the request. As human beings, we are biologically conditioned to accommodate requests for assistance. The compulsion is based upon the fact that our ancient ancestors knew that if they did not provide assistance when asked, the assistance would not be granted to them if requested at a later date. Each of us carries the genetics for this as a survival mechanism.

The importance of keeping the request easy and nonthreatening cannot be overemphasized. When individuals perceive that the assistance would imperil them or involve a cost to them, they are much less likely to accommodate such requests, especially with a stranger. Individuals who have close anchored bonds and relationships can rely on tougher requests, but, for the purpose of developing quick rapport and conversations, keep the requests "light."

A few years ago, I was on a work trip where I was going to provide training to agents in the art of elicitation. Elicitation is the act of inducing an individual to provide information without asking any direct questions related to the information that you seek and much too detailed a topic to be covered in this book.

For more on elicitation and the techniques required please contact me via my Website, http://www.peopleformula.com

While I was on this trip, I was traveling with another agent and friend who also was presenting in the course. My friend was intrigued and amazed that an individual was able to obtain so much information and great conversations from others with the use of these simple techniques. I had just demonstrated to him how easy it was to obtain personal information from a gentleman by the name of Albert at our rental car counter.

The next morning, I met my friend in the hotel lobby where a free continental breakfast was offered to guests. We had agreed the night before to meet at the breakfast buffet before going to the location for the training. When we sat down, my friend asked if the techniques worked with everyone. I elaborated that they are specifically designed to be effective on all human beings based upon our evolutionary biology. I added that each of our individual responses to the techniques is affected not only by the context of the situation and the skills of the individual using the techniques but also the most important unknown, the individual experiences of those we choose to interact with. Based upon an individual's life experiences the techniques will be more or less effective because of free will and choice. Great practitioners of these skills must be patient and continue to be accommodating of others if they hope to become a master conversationalist and rapport builder.

Each of us had gotten up, selected some items from the buffet and returned to our table to eat. While taking a much needed sip of coffee, my friend placed a challenge before me. He challenged me to elicit a good conversation from the very next person that walked into the breakfast room before we left for our daily presentations. My friend also added that I was to obtain personal information to maintain contact after we departed. I agreed.

Within a few minutes, a young woman walked in who looked to be close to my age. I had already strategized the first steps in the process of utilizing artificial time constraints, accommodating nonverbals, and a slower rate of speech. I also had planned on my sympathy theme in advance.

I have learned over years of utilizing these tools, as well as having to interview and speak to hundreds if not thousands of people, that it is vitally important to not give the impression that I have any romantic agenda or purpose to my conversation; my wife especially appreciates that. The very instant an individual believes you have romantic motives, the whole purpose of the interaction changes. Most often, the individual with whom you are chatting will quickly try to disengage and most likely not ever want to engage with you again.

The theme I always like to use is doing something special for my wife. I have learned that just mentioning you are married is not enough. Talking about your children is not enough. When I have tried those conversational techniques in the past, I have found that mentioning wives and children is often-times not enough to keep an individual from thinking you are "hitting on them." However, when I have mentioned that I want to do something very special for my wife, it demonstrates that not only am I married but that I think a great deal about her and our relationship. This technique and theme typically leave no doubt in the mind of the individual with whom you are speaking that you do not have romantic intentions.

The young woman claimed a table a across the room from my friend and me, placed her things on an empty chair at her table, and proceeded up to the buffet. The buffet included a number of hot and cold breakfast items, such as eggs, bacon, potatoes, breakfast breads, and cereals. I noted that this buffet didn't include anything particularly sweet. The breakfast room wasn't overly large and there were about 7-9 tables that accommodated up to four people. Each table was relatively close to the buffet, which was placed out on tables across one of the walls. It was pretty easy to hear conversation from the buffet at each table. I watched the woman as my friend watched me, wondering how I was going to approach this young woman and not seem like I was hitting on her. I watched the woman, trying to identify a third-party reference with which to initiate the conversation. As I mentioned earlier in the book, a third-party reference is a topic used to initiate that isn't too personal about the individual targeted for the discussion. The topic also is not about you. Individuals typically do not like talking to strangers about either of these topics, at least not in the first few seconds.

Unfortunately, I was not able to discern an appropriate third-party reference but I did take note of the fact that she had filled her plate with some of the buffet but still seemed to be searching for something. I noted that her plate had eggs, bacon and toast. Following a few minutes of regarding the table with a troubled look, she sat down by herself and began to eat.

I had noted to myself that I thought it was unusual for a breakfast buffet like this one not to have anything sweet, such as cinnamon rolls, scones, or pastries. I thought that maybe that was what she was looking for. Regardless, I identified those items as good third-party references to use.

Following my observations, I finalized my strategy for opening the dialogue and initiated my plan. I looked at my friend and told him to watch and we'll see what happens. I walked up to the buffet, grabbed another plate and began regarding the buffet. Like the young woman, I stood and looked a little puzzled. I ensured that I was within eyesight of her, but I kept my body facing at an angle to her. I looked over my shoulder and spoke across the room to my friend, "Hey, can you believe they don't have any cinnamon buns? It's crazy, I need my sugar fix." I made the statement with a good natured non-threatening smile. My friend looked at me, smiled, and merely shrugged. The young woman also looked up and smiled at me. I gave a very brief smile back, turned away, and went back to sit down.

When I sat down, my friend looked at me and said, "That's it? Where is the great conversation?" I told him to be patient it was coming. I went on to say that I had to desensitize her toward our presence and demonstrated that we were not overly interested in her, but the third-party reference, cinnamon buns. He nodded and said, "Ok, so what next?" "Patience," I said. "Great conversationalists have patience and wait for the right opportunity to capitalize on opportunities that are natural and not ones that are forced."

About ten minutes later, the young woman got up and walked over to the coffee dispensers. I again nodded to my friend and said, "Here we go, let's see if she is ready to have a chat today." I grabbed my coffee cup and approached a coffee dispenser next to hers and began to pour some for myself. My body was facing the coffee dispenser and not her as I stated offhandedly, "The buffet is really nice, but can you believe there is nothing sweet on that line?" The young woman turned toward me and smiled as she said, "I know, I was looking for a cheese Danish. I try to eat healthy but enjoy a treat now and then when I travel." The young woman looked as though she was willing to have a much greater conversation, but I decided to let her desire for a chat build a little more so that I could clearly establish that I didn't have any romantic interests or ulterior motives. I simply smiled and said, "That sounds good too, oh well." I gave a quick non-threatening smile and returned to my seat with my friend. My friend said again, "So that was the great conversation?" I said, "No, wait for it...."

The young woman returned to her seat and took out the morning paper to read as she was sipping her coffee. My friend and I finished our breakfasts and prepared to leave. I picked up my brief-case and prepared to leave, implied artificial time constraint. I walked by her table and she looked up. I looked at my friend and said, "Maybe I can ask her." My friend looked at me in a quizzical way and said, "oooookay." I kept my body angled slightly away and said with a grin and with a playful type of conversational banter, "I'm very sorry to bother you. My friend and I have to leave in a second to go to work. He claims to be a great gift idea guy but he is failing miserably." The young woman smiled as my friend caught on to the conversation and playfully added, "You just have no ability." I responded "You're probably right."

The young woman was still smiling but looking a bit puzzled. I quickly informed her that my wife and I were about to celebrate a special wedding anniversary, and I was trying to get her something really special. I offered, "I am at a real loss. I was hoping that you could help me with a few quick ideas." The woman smiled broader and said, "I'll try. How many years has been for you two?" Over the course of the next 15 minutes, the young woman, Julia, gave me some really great advice and ideas for anniversary gifts. Along the way, I also learned that her husband also was in law enforcement and that they had been married for a similar amount of time. They also had two children and one was a child with special needs. My friend who was with me also has a child with special needs, so they immediately had a common interest. Julia and I also had a love for country music. All of us departed for our day having felt better for having met each other.

I gained a significant amount of information about Julia in those 10-15 minutes. The wonderful technique of using the assistance or sympathy theme continued to be highlighted throughout the week. My friend and I saw Julia every morning at breakfast, and every morning she had another idea for me and the anniversary. She always started the conversation with how bad she felt she couldn't help me more, and I kept validating her ideas by researching each of them on my own so that she didn't feel like I was wasting her time. Between both work and the work of making better conversation and friends with Julia, it was an exhausting week. In the end, my favorite idea was to take my wife horseback riding, just the two of us and a guide. My wife loves horseback riding, and I did just that for her when I got home.

Hopefully, by now, you are recognizing that each of these techniques is very common and each of us utilizes them each day and in each moment of our lives. The purpose of going through these techniques here is to demonstrate to you what you are doing right when it goes well and why. Once you have an understanding of what these techniques are, you can plan and use them much more proactively in your life. Attending a get together or even just walking around shopping with a plan on how to talk with and engage people will give you a great sense of empowerment, connection, and understanding of others. These actionable behavioral skills can then be applied to every aspect of your professional life as well. Whether communicating with co-workers or trying to build to a sale, these are the techniques that ultimately win the day by demonstrating to the other individual, "It's not all about me."

Technique 5: Ego Suspension

Have you ever heard someone who made a false statement and NOT corrected them? Suspending an individual's ego is probably the most challenging, as well as effective techniques out of all ten that we will cover together. The ego is directly linked to so many of our interpersonal interactions, if not all of them. Human beings are genetically coded to be self-centered, or ego-centric, for our survival. When our ancient ancestors were a hunter-gatherer society, if an individual did not look after his or her own needs in those harsh environments, the chances of passing along the genes to offspring were pretty low. Suspending our individual ego is the most difficult because of our genetics. Conversely, it is one of the best techniques to utilize when an individual chooses to have a positive interaction and attain rapid rapport.

The most effective illustrator of this technique reminds me of a road rage incident I faced not too long ago. I was driving back from a long endurance run I had completed in the mountains of Virginia. The car ride home was about three hours and, after spending most of the day running 32 miles, I was very tired. My goal was simple, get home safely and eat pizza with my wife and two children. I was about 10-15 minutes from home and traveling in a congested part of Fredericksburg when I happened upon a scene that many of us have faced at one time or another. I was driving in a through lane while a left turn lane was partially backed up into the through lane. The tail end of the last car in the left-hand-turn lane was hanging out into my lane a bit, and I made the decision to just swerve to continue through. That's when it happened.

As soon as I swerved, I heard a horn blaring in my ear. I glanced to my right and saw a large four-door pickup truck with a very angry middle-aged man staring down at me giving me "the finger." I also noticed that the man had what looked like a 12-year-old girl as a passenger in his back seat. I surmised that the young girl was probably his daughter and thought to myself that he would probably gain his composure rapidly because of her. I was wrong.

I am going to digress at this point in the story for a moment because my initial lack of reaction requires a bit of an explanation. My lack of giving the man "the finger" back was not because of a higher plane of thinking or any sense or moral altruism. In fact, I had done just that a number of years earlier when I was first assigned as a new FBI agent in Manhattan, New York.

Following my new agent training in Quantico, Virginia, I was assigned to the FBI field office in Manhattan, New York. I was a brand new agent, as well as a Naval Academy graduate and a Marine Corps captain. This recipe for egocentrism was very high. In hindsight, there is no doubt I thought it was all about me. Within the first two weeks of my assignment, I remember walking down to my vehicle parked on Thomas Street. (An agent had to get into the office at around 5AM in order to get such a good spot so close to the office.) I got into my vehicle, turned the ignition, and drove up to the intersection of Church and Thomas and waited for the light to turn green. (FBI agents are issued a handgun, handcuffs, pepper spray, and an expandable baton. On this particular day, all I had with me were my gun and handcuffs, a mistake I didn't make again.)

While waiting for the light to turn from red to green, a New York bicycle messenger sped in front of my vehicle on his way to deliver his next package to a client. The messenger looked to be well over six feet tall and was covered in muscle from what looked like years of riding the streets of New York City delivering packages. He also had a very thick linked chain slung across his body for locking up his bicycle at each location while he went into a building to deliver his goods.

The bike messenger must have figured that I looked like an easy target, was too far into the intersection or both, because he looked down at me in my vehicle, sneered and gave me "the finger." Since I was still in a very "all about me" mode and full of the idea of myself and the all important "FBI guy" I did what any other fool would have done... I gave him "the finger" back as I said to myself, "Screw you too buddy, I'm an FBI guy." This is the time when life got interesting.

Just as the messenger whizzed by and I returned the one finger salute, the light turned green and I went through the intersection to begin my battle to the West Side Highway and my long journey home from the southern part of Manhattan to the suburbs. I was making my way to the next intersection and stop-light when I noticed a strange and somewhat terrifying sight in my rearview mirror, the bike messenger was chasing me, and he was closing in on me fast. The first thought that entered my mind after "oh #@$%" was that this guy is going to kick my ass if he catches me. I then remembered that all I had in the car with me was my handgun. The next thought that flashed through my mind was what the front page of one the New York newspapers would say the next morning if I had an altercation with the bike messenger that involved my weapon. I decided my best course of action was to run away and run fast.

I think I may have slightly exceeded the speed limit and possibly a few stop-lights in my attempt to make it to the highway with a speeding bicycler in pursuit. Luckily, I made it to the highway and my last glimpse of the messenger in my rearview mirror was of him turning onto the highway as well looking determined to "get me." This incident is still burned into my brain and, as a result, I never have flashed a vulgarity at another motorist.

Back in Fredericksburg, Virginia, all these memories went through my mind as I decided not to give Mr. Road Rage a vulgar gesture. My objective was to get home. To achieve my objective, I would consciously think through the next 10-15 minutes, which now included deescalating a road rage incident. My initial inclination was to demonstrate to Mr. Road Rage that he was overreacting and he was wrong. One way I thought of doing this was to make a vulgar gesture. Other ways I have witnessed include flashing a badge, staring down the individual, back, yelling at the other vehicle, and even getting out of the vehicle for an altercation. All of these actions and many other are nothing more than egos battling for supremacy without much regard for the consequences or objectives.

Mr. Road Rage got behind me, immediately put his bright lights on, and got within 1-2 inches of my rear bumper. As I was driving with Mr. Road Rage clearly fixated on me my wife called on my cell phone. I put my earpiece in and heard her asking about how far away from home I was so she could order pizza for me and our two children. I informed her that I was only about 10 minutes away, but it may take a few more minutes because I had a road rage guy following me. My wife let out a little shriek over the phone and passed along to me the instruction I always have given her in case of such an incident. My wife told me to drive to the nearest police station and seek assistance. I chuckled and told her that as good as I may be at times at suspending my ego, the former Marine and FBI agent did not allow for this and that I was not going to pull into a police station seeking help. I could imagine the conversation if I had. "Hi, I'm an FBI agent and armed and there is a road rage guy bothering me, HELP!" I do, however, encourage this response from any of you that may encounter these radical situations. Individuals will generally deescalate their anger as the police station comes into view. Safety is always paramount. Never fuel an emotionally high-jacked situation.

I informed my wife not to worry that I would use my skills to try to deescalate the situation. Following the conversation with my wife, I set my objectives. I wanted to get home, eat pizza, and have Mr. Road Rage calm down and go home safe as well. Once the objective is set, executing the plan comes down to how to communicate with those individuals impacted by your objectives. My first step was to try and look as nonverbally nonthreatening as possible. I tried to not look "challenging" to the Road Rage guy. I kept my chin angle down, elbows down on the steering wheel and got into the accommodating right-hand lane. Mr. Road Rage was not impressed with my attempts and stayed right behind me, white knuckles on the steering wheel and glaring at me.

Mr. Road Rage stayed with me for approximately 10 minutes through a few turns and was very obviously following me and not letting go of his anger. He was still looking for a

45

confrontation. As I approached the next stop light, he pulled into the lane immediately to my left and was still glaring at me with white knuckles on his steering wheel. I decided I needed to elevate my attempts at ego suspension. As the man glared down at me, I turned my head towards him and, with a very sheepish, contrite smile, I simply mouthed the words, "I'm sorry." The impact was immediate and impressive. Mr. Road Rage's nonverbal demeanor immediately melted, and he lowered his passenger side window. I saw that he was deescalating his hostility and felt it safe to lower my window as well. Once the window was lowered, Mr. Road Rage pointed his finger at me as he exclaimed, "It's idiots like you who cause accidents!" I continued to keep my ego suspended as I received the verbal abuse. My response was simple and contrite, "I know; I said I was sorry." I cannot begin to explain the internal turmoil I had as a former Marine as well as FBI agent to utter such words when I felt HE was the individual in the wrong for his behavior, but I kept my focus on the objective. After my statement, Mr. Road Rage looked positively perplexed and more nonverbal melting was happening. He physically looked as though he were deflating. Mr. Road Rage then gestured to his daughter in the back seat as he stated, "I have my daughter in the back seat." now realized that his consternation with my driving habits was most likely induced because he felt that his daughter's well being was threatened by my behavior. Regardless of my revelation as to "why," I continued my ego suspension theme as I said, "I know, I have children too… haven't you ever made a mistake?" Mr. Road Rage looked positively exhausted and amazed at this final statement. He clearly was anticipating confrontation and what he got was someone who was agreeing with him… "ego suspension." Mr. Road Rage looked at me after my final statement and said, "Well… God bless you and you

46

driving." The light turned green and he drove away without further incident.

Suspending your ego is nothing more complex than putting other individuals' wants, needs, and perceptions of reality ahead of your own. Most times, when two individuals engage in a conversation, each patiently waits for the other person to be done with whatever story he or she is telling. Then, the other person tells his or her own story, usually on a related topic and often times in an attempt to have a better and more interesting story. Individuals practicing good ego suspension would continue to encourage the other individual to talk about his or her story, neglecting their own need to share what they think is a great story. Human beings are not genetically coded to care as much about others and their stories as much as they care about their own. Self-centeredness is genetically coded in each of us because, without it, our ancestors would not have survived. Common etiquette and courtesy dictates that individuals be given equal time to share their own story of the events in their own life. Those individuals who allow others to continue talking without taking their own turn are generally regarded as the best conversationalists. These individuals are also sought after when friends or family need someone to listen without judgment. They are the best at building quick and lasting rapport.

My encounter with Mr. Road Rage is an excellent yet small example of ego suspension. In this case, what I believed to be my reasons as well as my own perception of the events did not matter. All that mattered to Mr. Road Rage was to prove he was correct in a very self-centered way. He was so emotionally high-jacked he did not have a larger set of objectives, like safety for himself or his daughter. Thinking clearly, setting objectives, and suspending your ego in furtherance of the set objectives is invaluable in any interpersonal engagement.

Technique 6: Validate Others

Whether you deny it or not, you want to be accepted and liked. From the first time a child begins conversing with his or her parents they are seeking approval for their actions and thoughts. Parents are continually reinforcing that there is a right way and a wrong way of doing just about everything. From an early age, each of us has sought the validation that we are accepted, and it continues right into adulthood. As with each of the needs and techniques we are covering, the degree to which an individual requires validation varies, but one thing is certain, each of us feels good when we are validated.

Validation comes in many forms. I have identified three types of validation. Each is very effective and can be used as the situation requires. The following are the three forms of validation, and they can be used independently or, to great effect, intertwined with each other:

Validation Technique 1: Listening

The simplest validation that can be given to another individual is simply listening. The action doesn't require any proactive effort aside from the incessant need each of us has to tell our own story. Validation is effective because it releases dopamine to the brain's pleasure centers. This is the same chemical reaction that takes place after drinking an alcoholic beverage, taking risks, or eating a great piece of chocolate. Think of a time when either you or someone you were speaking with started out a conversation saying they had to go in a few minutes and didn't disengage the conversation for quite some time after. I would venture to guess that if you think back to the reason why, it was because the person who stayed was being extremely well validated. In essence, the release of the dopamine from the validation was causing the individual to override cognitive thinking in exchange for feeling good.

In my job in the FBI, I have had the privilege of working with a great number of individuals considered confidential human sources. These individuals provided extremely valuable information, access, and insight into situations that directly impacted our national security and foreign relations.

I worked with a confidential human source while assigned to the New York City FBI office who had been helping the FBI and the United States for over thirty years before I was introduced to him, and we started working together on numerous counterintelligence operations. I remember sitting with him every few weeks eating our favorite Chinese food while I listened to him talk about all his past adventures helping the FBI and all about the 15 agents who he had worked with before me. I would sit and listen to him without saying much but a few encouraging words to keep him speaking for up to four hours. When the individual had finally finished what was on his mind, I would discuss what I came to for about ten minutes. The relationship was very strong and our success together was exceptional. Why? The reason was he felt validated.

The example above is one of hundreds of instances we all have had when the simple act of listening produces amazing results. The difficulty most of us have is keeping from interjecting our own thoughts, ideas, and stories during the conversation. True validation coupled with ego suspension means that you have no story to offer, that you are there simply to hear theirs.

When I run one of my courses for FBI agents, and I discuss validation and ego suspension and how effective they are, I am typically asked what the student should say if they are asked a question they are uncomfortable answering. I tell them that if they are properly validating and suspending his or her ego, no one will ask you any questions, and, if they do, they are simply trying to be polite. I instruct them to quickly bounce the conversation back to them, and they will continue talking. I haven't had a student yet say it hasn't worked. They are always amazed how much individuals simply want to talk and be listened to.

I and most others in my line of work are always amazed about how our confidential human sources like us better than most other people in our lives, such as friends, family, and colleagues. That is because many of us will put a friend on hold to take another call or tell them we have to go when they need someone to listen to them. A great conversationalist and rapport builder will put the entire focus on the other individual. When we aren't anxious to tell our own story, we also tend to listen and hear better. We also will remember details that we otherwise would not.

I had worked with an excellent confidential source and human being when I was working in one of my assigned field offices. He was a highly educated man and had worked on a nuclear program for a non-friendly foreign country. He became a tremendous resource for the FBI and others. He also gave classes to newer agents on how to communicate and recruit their own confidential human sources like him. The confidential human source had a checklist of what not to do that he had experienced over his years of working with the FBI. The number one thing on his list was that an agent should not take out his cell phone and either take a call or start e-mailing or texting when meeting with the source. He went on to say that it demonstrated that there are many other things more important than the source. That is a really bad message to send anyone in your life whom you value.

Validation Technique 2: Thoughtfulness

Thoughtfulness is probably the most commonly used of the validation techniques but in a limited manner. I want to emphasize it here because I have found through my practical application of these techniques, as well as study of personality types, that few people naturally use this to its fullest potential and, most of the time, we don't realize when it is being used; all we know is we really like the person who gives it.

My wife happens to be one of those individuals who naturally places the needs, wants, and welfare of others above her own. She is constantly asking if you need anything. She always says "Be careful." She always will prepare something for you to eat before she prepares something for herself. My wife has this natural, beautiful gift that I only recently understood and recognized. I say that because I never consciously took count of the number of times a day she says a comforting or kind word or showed interest in the well-being of me, our children, and others. I tried counting on a few occasions, and I lost count after 50.

Demonstrate thoughtfulness in your actions and, more important, your words to every individual in your life, and predict those relationships will greatly be enhanced. The effect is easily used on strangers as well. I began carrying both hand sanitizer as well as chewing gum wherever I go. While standing in a line at a store or sitting chatting with strangers or friends, I will take out either and offer it to another individual first. The positive effect is immediate and the individual is generally very receptive to conversation.

Validation Technique 3: Validate Thoughts and Opinions

Most human beings are very self-centered. We are biologically bred to be self-centered as a survival mechanism. That is why when in stressful survival type situations, our natural inclinations are to take care of our own safety first then the needs of others. That is also why when we witness what we consider heroic acts of others, we are recognizing how some individuals have defied their own genetics and biology and made a choice to put others' needs and wants first. These are considered admirable qualities because they go against our innate egocentric survival mechanisms.

Validating the thoughts and opinions of others is very powerful but can also be very difficult because of our innate need to correct others and the difficulty we have suppressing our own egos. Human beings naturally make a connection with others who "think like we do." Consider the fact that if every human being actually validated the thoughts and opinions of others, there would be no world conflicts. The beauty of all of these tools and techniques is that they are all part of our individual choices.

I have found one of the most effective methods for getting individuals to do what I want them to do is to have them come up with my idea then I validate their idea. For example, a few years ago, I had a brand new confidential human source was working with. I knew before one of our meetings that wanted him to help me on a project that would require him to report on situations surrounding one of our country's political adversaries that had been targeting our country and committing corporate espionage. In these situations, I find it is always much better to first understand the other individual's point of view, then validate his or her point of view and build upon it with my ideas.

While at the meeting, I asked my source, "So, what do you think about country X?" His response was perfect. He said, "I think they are doing great harm to the United States." I responded, "That's an interesting point of view, why do you think that?" Following his response, I validated his thoughts again, and then asked him what he thought we could do about it. The entire dialogue and process was centered on my source's ideas and me validating them to have him take action.

It is very easy to utilize this technique anywhere, including work. I have often used the same technique with colleagues. Empower those around you with choices, albeit choices that you have offered, but in the end, the decision is theirs. For example, I was tasked with developing a new course of instruction. I did not readily see the need for the new course and thought it to be unnecessary. I knew that if I didn't take the initiative, the course would be developed without my input. Instead of saying, "I don't think that is a good idea," or "We don't need to do that," I said, "That is a very good idea that I hadn't thought of. I see the merit of it. Let me come up with a few ideas for you to choose from." I then had my colleagues on my side and not defensive but open to the options I brought them. Within a few hours, I proposed options for implementing the idea. Each of the options, though, was completely my idea and I would be satisfied with any of them. I presented the choices, and we decided on one as a course of action. This is what you call a "win-win" scenario, all of my own choices through the validation of someone else's ideas.

Technique 7: Ask... How? When? Why?

I have had total strangers tell me their deepest darkest secrets from really unusual sexual experimentations, to obsessions with designer blue jeans and everything in the middle. A key step to strengthening the emotional connection in any relationship is to anchor or solidify the relationship with "how, when, and why" questions.

One of the key concepts that every great interviewer or conversationalist knows is to ask open ended questions. Open ended questions are ones that don't require a simple yes or no answer. They are generally questions that require more words and thought. Once the individual being targeted in the conversation supplies more words and thought, a great conversationalist will utilize the content given and continue to ask open ended questions about the same content. The entire time, the individual being targeted is the one supplying the content of the conversation.

For example, in my story about the older gentleman that I chatted with in the Panera restaurant, I utilized all the techniques discussed so far to open the dialogue and conversation about what he thought was an appropriate age for girls to start dating. The gentleman leaned back in his chair, put a big smile on his face and said, "Well, I do have two daughters, one 23 and the other 25." I replied, "Ahh, so I have an expert." He chuckled and said that he wasn't an expert but he did have some experience. I then asked him the open ended question based on exactly what he said. I asked, "Please tell me about your experience." The key words here are "please," which hits on the sympathy theme and "your experience" is merely follow-up with information he had already released. It is very important to listen to the content that the other individual supplies and thread from that content using open ended questions.

My friend at the Panera restaurant went on to discuss that he didn't like the first boyfriend that his oldest daughter brought home. Threading with the provided content, I asked, "Why?" The gentleman elaborated, describing how the young man didn't display much respect for him by the way he strolled into his house and tried to avoid eye contact and conversation with him. I asked my friend if he thought this was maybe a generational difference. My friend thought for a minute and said that maybe it was generational.

By asking a generational type of question, I was attempting to introduce another line of conversation from the original based upon the first. This is called threading the conversation. I followed up with another open ended question that would, hopefully, give me even more content to work with. asked my friend, "What was it like when you were growing up and allowed to date?" This type of open ended anchoring question will test the new relationship dialogue and give you a quick idea about how far and deep you can venture in these quick conversations. If the answer is quick and short, do not pursue it any longer; if it tends to be a bit longer, you have something to work with. In this particular case, my friend continued to elaborate about where he grew up and the type of values his parents had instilled in him. He also went on to discuss his three brothers and one sister.

Following a few more "how, when, and why," he went on for 20-30 minutes about all aspects of his growing up and his family life, including how he recently lost his mother and how his father was beginning to show signs of dementia. The things people will share when given the opportunity is truly remarkable. This technique would not have been nearly as effective if I was waiting my turn to interject my own stories. Remember, ego suspension is critical.

There are a few more techniques associated with asking "how, when, and why" that I feel are equally important that you should attempt to incorporate:

- Minimal encouragers
- Reflective questions
- Emotional labeling
- Paraphrasing
- Pauses
- Summarize

The first is the use of **minimal encouragers**. These are simple head nods or verbal confirmations that you are paying attention and listening, such as "uh huh," "yes," "I understand," etc. Using your accommodating nonverbal communication style here is very effective and congruent with this technique. I need to add a word of caution however; doing this insincerely or too much can lead to the individual viewing you as uncaring and cold.

The second technique is another form of questioning but without having to think of a question or a way to get the person to tell you more; it is **reflective questioning**. These are really fun, but take some practice if you are not familiar with using them. I have personally found them to be absolutely terrific and easy once you are accustomed to using them. For example, in my dialogue with my friend above, at one point, he described how the young man who came over to date his daughter didn't have much respect for him. If my friend had stopped there, and I wanted him to elaborate without seeming to pushy, I could simply repeat what he just said, "He didn't have much respect for you?" By restating what he just said but as a question, the individual becomes compelled to elaborate more. The technique of reflective questioning uses some sympathy because you need help in understanding something. The technique also touches on the human characteristic of wanting to mentor and teach others. Most human beings are genetically wired to be responsive to these techniques.

I use this with my children as well. Not too long, ago my daughter came home from school and informed my wife and me that she wanted to wear makeup to a school dance. Instead of badgering her with questions of my choosing, I allowed her to explain in more detail first by using reflective questioning. I was curious about the school dance, so I said, "School dance?" Following my daughters explanation of the dance, I said, "Make up?" She then elaborated on what she wanted to do regarding wearing makeup. These opening reflective questions allowed my daughter to feel in control and as if she was being listened to Then, when I introduced other ideas and considerations, she tended to be more receptive. And, yes, ultimately, she decided not to wear makeup to the school dance.

Emotional labeling is the next technique. This can be very powerful technique, especially in instances where someone is displaying a great deal of emotion. Discovering the causes of those emotions can lead to rich engagements. I generally don't use this technique unless I see individuals who appear to have had a rough day. It is useful because I have found that the general third-party reference and other techniques are not as effective when individuals feel distraught or just in an overall bad mood. I have found that having an open ear in these situations allows the individual to feel better for talking, and, generally, you can't get them to be quiet once they start.

My most striking recent example of the power of emotional labeling involves me and a friend. For a short period of time, my friend / colleague and I traveled around the country teaching some of these techniques to FBI field agents. My friend and I would instruct different blocks of instruction based upon our individual skills. On one trip to Chicago, my friend had asked me how I ended up having such in-depth conversations with total strangers. I described to him the concept of asking, "How? When? and Why?" as well as emotional labeling. We had just finished our dinner that evening and were sitting in the hotel lounge where we were staying, watching a sporting event on TV.

My friend challenged me with having one of these deep conversations with the very next person who came into the lounge and sat near us. I agreed, but I also challenged him with the same task. Not three seconds later a woman who looked to be in her late 50s to early 60s came in and sat down next to me. She looked defeated and exhausted. The woman quickly ordered a glass of wine and began staring at the wall. I glanced over at my friend who just smiled at me. He then had a similar woman sit next to him. I chuckled to myself and began to think about how to open the conversation.

I began by matching her nonverbal behavior and stared at the same wall. A few minutes later I stated openly, "Stressful day, huh?" The woman glanced at me over her shoulder, and I kept my position facing the wall so as to not be threatening. She said, "You have no idea." I simply nodded in agreement. We were both staring ahead when I noticed an unusual piece of decorative art on the wall. I ordered a glass of wine like hers and stated, "What do you think that represents?"

The techniques I chose started with a bit of emotional labeling to break the ice, and then I backed off and later interjected a third-party reference about the art. The woman responded that she didn't exactly know but began to offer some of her thoughts about it. I then asked her about why her day was stressful.

We had already been chatting about the art for 5-10 minutes, so the woman felt comfortable enough to start sharing that she was the office manager for five local buildings and that she had a horrible day dealing with difficult tenants. The conversation with her lasted for another hour. At one point, we went back to discussing the art on the wall. She informed me she got into art during the time she was institutionalized for having nervous breakdown. I was still amazed that she never once asked me about what I did for a living or any questions about myself. Remember, if you don't try to interject your content, people generally won't ask. Most people would rather tell their own stories rather than listen to yours.

I had just about had my fill of the conversation when I glanced over to see my friend. To my amazement, he glanced over at me with a blank stare. I looked around to the woman I was speaking to and noted that she had tears running down her face. He merely nodded at me, then at the exit. We excused ourselves from our respective conversations and went to the elevator bank to head up to our respective rooms. I asked him, "What happened? He told me that he had done exactly what I said to do. The next thing he knew she was telling him about her divorce and got extremely emotional. He didn't know what to say or do but felt really bad. We both witnessed the power of emotional labeling, as well as the effect of suspending our own need to talk about ourselves.

Paraphrasing is the next technique that demonstrates to the other person that you are paying attention. It is also great at helping you remember the content of the conversation for recall later. I remember once sitting on a plane next to a woman named Gail. Gail went on to discuss how she lived with her father because she is a single mom. She had given birth to her first son when she was sixteen and still in high school. I didn't sit in judgment of the choice she had made but validated how tough it must have been and what a challenge it must have been to raise her son. Gale went on to tell me that she had another son before graduating high school but that she was very proud of her boys. Her eldest son was starting his senior year of college and doing very well, and her youngest had just enlisted in the Marine Corps. I again commended her on the parenting she gave her boys.

I remember about half-way through the conversation I paraphrased what she had been talking to me about for the last hour. I said, "So, please, correct me where I am wrong; you gave birth to your first son when you were sixteen, your mother left you and your father. Your father had you stay at home and helped you raise your sons. You and your boyfriend were going

63

to get married but then he ran off. Your father is a hardworking farmer and taught your boys the value of good hard work, and you were able to finish school as they worked the farm." Gale just looked at me in amazement and said, "Wow, you were actually listening?"

People have gotten so used to people not giving them their full attention that when you do, it is the most wonderful and cheapest gift and rapport builder on earth. Paraphrasing can be both an excellent tool at establishing that you are listening, and it also can serve as a reflective type of questioning but on a much broader scale. Following my paraphrasing with Gale, she elaborated more just as in a reflective question. Similar to paraphrasing, this technique is also fantastic for remembering details. For example, I am sitting here writing all these anecdotes to illustrate my points without any notes on these events. No matter what the time lapse has been, I remember them as vividly as the day they happened. Meanwhile, my wife gets on me to remember what the kids after-school activities are for the day. Thinking about it, I should probably use this more at home.

Interlaced with all these techniques is the placement of **pauses**. Creating a pause in a conversation can serve two purposes. The first is to create a break in the dialogue so you can think about what you want to say next, rather than continue to go on without thought. The second purpose is to create that slightly awkward silence that hopefully the other person will fill with his or her own content. Once he or she provides more content, you will have more items to ask, "How? When? and Why?" about.

Finally, use a **summary** at the end of the conversation. Similar to the other techniques, the summary serves a few purposes. First, it will act like paraphrasing in that it wil demonstrate to the other person that you were listening. Second, like paraphrasing, the summary will help you remember the content of the conversation for future conversations. Finally, the summary is great if there were any favors asked or commitments made. The summary eliminates any confusion on these points if they were not clear during the original discussion. Being clear about the content, obligations, or commitments made during the conversations keeps misunderstanding and potential hurt feelings later on at a minimum.

Asking "How? When? and Why?" is just another small part of the entire formula for interpersonal relationships. Executing these steps alone won't guarantee success. Each technique is woven within each other. This step is a very critical one, however, when trying to create more meaningful emotional anchors and trust with people. Human beings are constantly exploring whether they are being accepted for who they are. When a great conversationalist evokes stories, such as the ones described above, and does so without judgment and gives validation, the feeling of trust builds. Remember though, it is all about them and not you. Suspend your own ego and do not expect reciprocity in the form of asking about you or what you do or about the things that you think make you great. Some people may actually care, but more often they are more interested in themselves. Let them share.

Technique 8: Connect With Quid Pro Quo

Sometimes you have to give to get. Quid pro quo refers to the art of giving a little information about yourself to get a little from others. Out of all of the techniques, this one is the most subtle and if all of the others techniques are working effectively, might not be used at all.

In my experiences, there are really only two types of situations where I have utilized quid pro quo. The first and more common of the instances is when you attempt to converse with someone who is either very introverted, guarded, or both. The second instance is when the person you are conversing with suddenly becomes very aware about how much they have been speaking, and they suddenly feel awkward. In both instances giving a little information about you will help alleviate some of the issues.

A few years ago, I was on a flight from Washington, DC to Los Angeles and before I had gotten on the plane, I had decided that I wanted to try out a few more conversation techniques during the trip. I was very excited because I had just discovered using a "third-party reference" as a conversation starter. A "third party reference" is where you discuss something not about you or the other person to initiate a conversation.

I walked down the aisle and took my seat. Seated next to me against the window was a woman about my age. She was dressed like a business professional and was diligently reading some papers and materials. It appeared as though she was studying for something. As I sat down, I smiled at her and began contemplating my opening third-party reference line.

Following take off and our ascent to our cruising altitude, the woman took out a laptop computer and began working on that, as well as her notes. I thought that this was a good opportunity to use the laptop as a good third-party reference. I said, "Hi, I'm sorry to bother you, but I'm in the market for a new laptop and was wondering what you thought of yours?" The woman looked up at me sheepishly and said it was ok and went back to her working / studying. I was really disappointed that I wasn't able to strike up more of a conversation with that great third-party reference opener.

I quickly realized that a third-party reference alone may not be enough for some people. I decided that it might be effective if I divulge a little about myself first to make her feel safe. I also wanted to ensure that she didn't think I was going to talk at her for the five-hour flight. My next strategy was simple; I decided to match her nonverbally by taking out my laptop and working on it. I have numerous pictures of my children on my laptop, so I thought sharing a few pictures of my children first might be a good way to both demonstrate that I'm non-threatening as well as bringing in some potential other topics of conversation for later.

I let about an hour pass, then took out my laptop and began working on another article I had been contemplating. The woman continued her diligent attention to her own work. After about five minutes I pulled up a few photos of my two children when they were toddlers. I left them on the screen and said to the woman, "I'm sorry to interrupt you, but my wife sent me these photos of my kids this morning, and I just have to share them."

The woman leaned over and looked at my photos, and a big smile emerged on her face. I thought to myself, "I'm in!"

The woman commented that my children were very cute and asked me their ages. I told her and then added one or two more facts about their current interests. I then shifted the conversation back to her and asked her if she had any siblings. The woman said that she did and didn't offer more. I could tel quickly that I needed to offer even a little more quid pro quo and stated that it was really interesting because my two children are very close in age, 22 months, and enjoy many of the same things. I went on to inquire about her experience. Finally the woman began to speak a bit more about her siblings and growing up in a small family in a Chicago suburb. I listened intently and utilized the "how, when, and why" techniques discussed in the las chapter. Following my validation of her content / conversation, politely left her to resume her studying. Remember, my intent i never to overwhelm but to slowly build trust through non threatening dialogue.

About another hour later, the drink and snack service ha come and gone. I politely offered assistance to hold things fc her and offered my tray space for her work so she could enjo her beverage without fear of spilling it on her laptop or work. A these techniques are part of gift giving that we will cover in th next chapter. I didn't attempt any conversation during thes times because I, again, did not want to seem pushy to someon who was obviously intent on studying and working.

Shortly following the drink service, the woman bega studying again. I decided it was a good time to again attempt third-party reference and see how far I could take it. We ha spent hours next to each other. I was very polite. I divulge personal information using quid pro quo, and I had been unobtrusive so far. I leaned slightly over to her and said, "I don't know what you are studying for, but, as far as I can tell, you will ace whatever test it is for." This very validating statement had the required effect. The woman smiled broadly and thanked me. She went on to tell me about the test she was studying for. She also went on to discuss that she was a network administrator for a large aerospace business and a great deal of other personal and professional information. The woman's name was Latania and we had a nice conversation for the last hour of the plane ride. The success of this engagement was not because of one technique alone, but because I remained flexible, used multiple techniques, and recognized early on that I was speaking with someone who was introverted, guarded, and definitely busy. Realizing these issues early helped me to use patience as well as quid pro quo to make her feel more comfortable with a dialogue. The key is not to speak about you too much. Remember, it is all about them, not you.

The second instance we might use quid pro quo is when the individual we are conversing with has that sudden look of, "Oh gosh, how much have I been talking?" This has happened to me on more than one occasion. Inevitably, when we are using these techniques effectively, the individuals we are speaking with will continue to speak uninterrupted for as long as you are willing to listen. Most often, they have no idea how much information they are giving up, and they also are oblivious that they are the only ones talking. As I have said before, all of the people I have taught these techniques to are dumbfounded with how little someone will ask about you if you keep the focus on them.

There are those occasions, however, when the person suddenly realizes that they have been going on and on about themselves. Usually, in those instances, they feel vulnerable because they tend to do a quick mental recap on all the deep content they have just revealed to someone they either just met or barely know. In those moments of realization, they tend to feel as if they were standing naked in front of you because of how much they have shared. The best way to keep this from happening is to sprinkle a little quid pro quo throughout the dialogue before it gets that far. In general, if you have been letting someone speak about themselves and it is going pretty good for about 15 minutes, think about interjecting one or two small quick lines about yourself. Keep this quick and light so that you don't shift the focus from them to you. The whole purpose here is to show that you are similar in your likes and interests and also make them feel as though they are not the only one speaking.

I remember one of the funniest instances I encountered was when I took a work-related trip to Miami a few years ago. I was staying at a great hotel in a higher class section of Miami and decided to have dinner at the hotel bar that evening after work. I generally like these environments when traveling because they offer great opportunities to practice these skills with both patrons, as well as the bar staff.

On this particular evening the bar was pretty slow. My waitress / bartenders name was Kristi. I ordered a Caesar salad for dinner. When Kristi brought out my salad, she asked if there was anything else she could get me. I am a bit weird about some food things, and I absolutely love spicy food... on everything. I asked Kristi if she could bring me some hot sauce for my salad

She gave me a quizzical look and brought me some. As I sprinkled the hot sauce over my salad she asked if I like hot salsa as well. I told her I did and that I really loved spicy food. These topics ended up being a great third-party reference to start with. Kristi then spent the next hour telling me all about how she makes the best salsa ever. She went on to tell me about her career in the hospitality industry, how she is almost done with her degree in the same, her boyfriend who is trying to become a state trooper, and all of their mutual dreams and aspirations. I remember after that first hour she looked at me with that "Uh, oh" look and said, "Oh my gosh, I can't believe how much I've been talking." It was really funny because as soon as she said it, I gave a very small amount of quid pro quo and she was off talking again. I was having such a fun time gleaning all types of information from her that I let the conversation go on for about three hours. I must have done a great job at validating her content because the next day when I went down for dinner, she handed me her and her boyfriend's secret salsa recipe she had copied down for me, along with a small jar of it they had made for me.

Out of all of the techniques we have discussed, I have found that quid pro quo is not the most common one I use, but it does become infinitely important when you encounter the two types of situations I described above. When you do find yourself in the type of situation where you are going to use the technique, ensure that you use it sparingly and only as much as needed and no more because the focus always must remain on the individual you are targeting and not yourself. As long as you are using quid-pro-quo for them and not you, the conversation will be a success.

Technique 9: Gift Giving (Reciprocal Altruism)

Most people would feel badly if they received a gift and forgot to say or send a thank you note to the giver. When someone does you a favor you most likely want to reciprocate with gratitude. Great rapport builders and conversationalists use this desire proactively during every conversation.

This technique, coupled with ego suspension, are the cornerstones for building great relationships. This is also the easiest technique to utilize, because gifts come in many forms, from non-material compliments, to tangible material gifts. Gift giving, or reciprocal altruism, is hardwired in our genetics.

Mankind's ancestors were hunters / gatherers. Being part of a hunter / gatherer society meant that when the hunters would go on a hunt, not all would be successful. The hunters would return to camp, and the ones that had success would either share or not share the food they had procured. The hunters that didn' share would likewise not have food shared with them, if they found themselves in the situation where they were unsuccessful or became sick or invalid. The hunters that shared or "gift gave," were taken care of and given food in reciprocity for the gifts of food that they gave earlier on. The genetics of the survivors were then passed on; in other words, gift giving or reciprocal altruism is in each of our genetic codes. Human beings in general have a compulsion to reciprocate gifts given. Social norms can often times enhance this desire, but regardless, it exists at the genetic level.

I generally will give either material or non-material gifts. Many of the techniques described before now are actually great examples of non-material gifts or the gift of "focus." Each of these types of gifts focuses on the other individual and doesn't possess any material substance. Keeping the focus on another person in this non-material manner releases the chemical dopamine in our brains to our pleasure center receptors and can generally give us good feelings. This can be a great gift and is often why these techniques work. People love to get gifts and the better the gift giver you are, the more people will want to be around you to get the gift of "focus."

When giving the gift of "focus" the individual receiving the gift may or may not be conscious of the gift they are receiving. Regardless, the desire to reciprocate remains strong. The best part about the gift of "focus" is that it tends to be inexpensive. Each of the stories I have told throughout this book have encompassed a degree of the gift of "focus." In all of my examples, the individuals I was interacting with were consciously unaware of the gift I was giving. They were reciprocating the gift by having a conversation with me, allowing me to photograph them in their boots, giving me sensitive personal information, walking away from road rage, or telling me their inner-most secrets. This next example was a non-material gift that I gave.

A few years ago, I was taking some advanced classes in psychology. There was an individual in my organization, Bill, who was in charge of the program that I was studying. I was constantly amazed at how dedicated Bill was at his job and how helpful and cheery he always was, despite the fact that he alone was in charge of managing 1200 people and their needs in the program. Bill kept me motivated and going even when I wanted to give up. I was very grateful to Bill for all he had done for me, even though it was a nonmaterial gift. I felt compelled to reciprocate the gift and I did so using the gift of focus like he had.

I wrote an article about Bill and the type of great leadership and help he was for the FBI's Law Enforcement Bulletin. The article described Bill and how anyone can be a leader from any position they hold. The article was published in the February, 2011 edition of the Law Enforcement Bulletin. was very excited when I told Bill about the article I wrote about him. I also informed his management about the article and how Bill had inspired me because of the great work ethic and leadership he uses every day.

Material gifts are similar to the gift of focus, but the individual generally knows he or she is receiving a gift because of the tangible nature of the gift. Although, the type of gift given may not immediately trigger recognition of a gift, the result of their need to reciprocate will be the same.

Everyone recognizes when someone gives them wrapped gift, but do you recognize when other material gifts are given? For example, I generally carry both hand sanitizer and breath mints with me. While standing in a line at a checkout counter, I may take my hand sanitizer out, and offer some to the person next to me before I take some myself. Even if they decline, they feel the need to reciprocate the offer of the gift. Most often, it is reciprocated in the willingness to converse. will do the same thing with breath mints. You would be amazed at how friendly and helpful people become when you offer them a small gift or token. The best time to give the gift is before the offer you one. Preemptive gift giving is great at facilitating future engagements.

On a recent trip to New York City, I decided to take the train from where I live in Virginia. I boarded the train with my small travel bag and typical arsenal of hand sanitizer, breath mints, and a host of other FBI lapel pins and trinkets that make great gifts. The seat next to me was empty when I first got on, but as the train made a few more stops a gentleman about my age sat down, took out a newspaper and began reading it. I didn't say anything, just sat there and read a book as well. A short while later he asked me if I knew where the lavatory was. I pointed to the front of the car and said I thought it was that way. He thanked me, and asked me to save his seat while he checked it out. A few minutes later he returned, stating that the lavatory was indeed that way.

My assistance to the gentleman was already considered to be a nonmaterial gift and he seemed grateful. When the gentleman returned, I decided to enhance the gift giving and offered him some hand sanitizer. He gratefully accepted some and thanked me. I allowed the man his space and I continued to read my book. Another short while later, the man said he was going to go to the snack car and asked again if I would watch his seat for him. I smiled and agreed. When he returned, he had a bag of chips and a chocolate chip cookie with a soda. When he finished his snack, I took out my breath mints, took one for myself and asked if he would like one. He again took one and thanked me.

Following the last gift, the man angled his body toward me, and said that he was very appreciative for how friendly and helpful I had been to him. He asked me where I was heading. I told him New York City. The gentleman told me he was also, and that he was the manager at a very high end steak house in Manhattan. He took out his business card, wrote a few words on it and handed it to me. The man instructed me to bring a guest and this card into his restaurant when I was in town, and he would ensure we enjoyed a great evening together on him. I was astonished and extremely grateful for such a wonderful gift. I thanked the gentleman profusely and dug into my bag and presented him with a small token of thanks in the form of an FBI Behavioral Analysis Program commemorative coin. I described to him the heraldry of the coin, and the meaning behind each symbol. Each of us was very grateful for the fine gifts, both material and immaterial that we exchanged that day.

The key to the success of the last story was that I started the gift giving, and did so without any expectation of reciprocity. When individuals give gifts or do kind deeds with an agenda at the forefront of their mind, it demeans the value of the gift, and has the appearance of insincerity. The key to being a successful gift giver is to manage your expectations and keep the focus on them.

Technique 10: Manage Expectations

Have you ever wondered why bad used car salesmen come across as sleazy? Or, by contrast, have you ever met someone that you felt immediately at ease with and felt like you could chat forever? There are people among us that can walk up to a known spy on the street, offer him a great opportunity to work for the United States, and do so with the greatest of ease and grace. One factor effecting these situations is the ability to manage expectations.

Every conversation or engagement with another human being has an agenda. Another definition of agenda might be objective or desired outcome. Sometimes the agenda is to sell you a used car. Sometimes the agenda is to share a secret. Other times, it is simply to make another person feel better. Regardless of the situation, whether it is an altruistic intention or not, there is an agenda. The individuals in life that are able to either mask their agenda or shift the agenda to something altruistic will have great success at building rapport.

For example, when my family and I were preparing to move from one state to another, we researched a number of different realtors before making our final decision. We interviewed each realtor and asked them a few simple questions. The most important question to us was, "Why do you like being a realtor?" The answer that my wife and I were looking for was, 'I enjoy being a realtor so that I can help families find their perfect home." If the realtor didn't answer with that response, they were already ruled out. If the realtor gave us the answer we were looking for, we followed up with, "How do you go about doing that?"

Most of the realtors that we interviewed gave the proper initial response, but the follow-up question elicited a myriad of responses. The realtor's response that we liked best included that he had grown up in our area. Our realtor, Chris, knew the area intimately, from the school systems to the zoning laws to the myriad of subdivisions and all their related issues. Chris was also knowledgeable about all the home builders for each subdivision. He went on to describe that he saw it as his responsibility to pass this knowledge onto us so that we can make the right choice for our family. I asked Chris if he ever gave his personal opinion. He said that he never does unless asked, and then he ensures that he explains his personal rationale for his choices so that we would be able to weigh it objectively against our own. Chris's main objective was to ensure our happiness. I asked him if this has been an effective business model for him. Chris stated that placing the client's needs above his personal sales objectives has been effective because, if he provides a client great service they will inevitably be happier and hopefully pass along a referral.

My wife and I like what we had heard from Chris, and decided to go with him and see if his actions backed up his words. A few weeks later we had seen a good many homes with him and he was true to his word. Chris was indeed 100% focused on our needs and wants. He didn't try to sell us higher priced homes that would bring him a greater profit. Chris did a great job of focusing on us, and managing his own personal expectations and agenda.

When we are able to shift or manage our expectations we reduce potential disappointment. When we are disappointed we sometimes get angry and may even hold grudges and get hurt feelings. These emotions are not conducive to healthy or long term relationships. These emotions are definitely not conducive to developing quick rapport. The best technique to avoid these emotions is to manage expectations. In the example above, Chris had the goal of selling a house. Some realtors will create objectives in order to accomplish this goal, such as make extra on a commission by selling a larger house. Chris decided to switch his objective to finding the perfect house for us. By managing his expectations and focusing on our needs rather than his own, Chris ensured our long-term loyalty and relationship. Needless to say, we were very happy because I have referred numerous people, as well as writing about him in this book.

I discovered the technique of shifting and managing expectations while working for the FBI in New York City. My job sometimes required me to walk up to individuals who didn't know me and who were known to be spying against the United States on behalf of another country. Then, I had to ask them if they would like to work for the United States government. These "approaches" were never as crude as I just described, but it gives you the general idea. I remember the very first time I was going to perform what we call a "pitch." I was extremely nervous for a number of reasons. I think the main reason was that if he were to agree to have a dialogue about the possibility; it was the equivalent in the intelligence world of winning the lottery. I remember I was so nervous because I was going to walk up to a stranger and ask a very sensitive question. About thirty minutes before I was going to "bump into him" on a street corner while he was out for a walk, I decided to shift my expectations as well as my perception. Instead of having the expectation of a yes or no answer from a complete stranger, I decided to think of him as

79

a friend I was about to provide an opportunity to. I let go of my expectation and hoped for a yes, and focused on making a proposal to him. This simple shift in my expectation lowered my anxiety greatly.

A few minutes later I encountered the gentleman and we had a wonderful conversation and quick rapport based upon all of the techniques I have described to you in this book. Managing my expectations ensured that I sounded and looked confident and calm while performing a very stressful task. This technique is important and crucial because all of the techniques before this one require you to not seem like a seedy used car salesman when having a conversation. If you can manage your expectation before an encounter and ensure the conversation is for their benefit and not yours, you will greatly enhance your chances for success.

I am going to dedicate the last part of this chapter to my wife and all the beautiful people in the world like her. I really discovered the need to manage expectations based upon my observations of her and the hurt feelings and frustrations she would sometimes have. My wife is one of those wonderful people who will ask you about your children, family, and everything that is going on in your life. She will naturally follow up each answer with the technique of "how, when, and why." My wife naturally has a suspended ego. In other words, she does a fantastic job at many of these techniques naturally, like I am sure many others do as well. The difference I noticed between her and I though was in our individual responses to individuals who don't ask about our family, children, or personal interests.

My wife sometimes has the unrealistic expectation that people would like to ask her about her family as much as she enjoys asking about theirs. Many times she would come away from conversations and express her hurt and frustration to me. When I was able to finally realize what was happening, I was able to explain to her this concept of managing expectations. My wife has an agenda when engaging in these conversations. Her agenda is to find out about the family and interests of others. To a lesser degree, her other agenda is to tell you about her family. As we have learned earlier, when a person is really good at using these techniques, the other person will keep talking and talking and never want to hear from you. This is what my wife was experiencing. I explained my observations to her. She looked at me after a minute of thought and said, "You're right, so what can I do?" I told her she can make a choice. The choice is simple, don't change what you are doing, but also don't expect people will reciprocate the family questions. Or, the other choice is to simply stop validating others as much as you do so your feelings are not as hurt.

My wife decided to continue to validate others because she does enjoy finding out about them and their families more than she likes sharing about hers. Now and then, she will encounter another person like her that will ask about our kids and our family. In these cases she is in pure heaven, because it was not expected and a wonderful gift. The best gifts are the unexpected ones.

Ultimately we can never predict the actions of others, no matter how skilled we are at these techniques. The surest way however of not being disappointed is to ensure that we manage our expectations before ever commencing an engagement. Along with managing our expectations, we need to keep the focus on the needs and the perception of the other person, because it really is not all about me.

Putting it all together:

Let's go through the ten techniques to refresh our memories. This is also a good page to mark so that you can refer to it quickly before any encounter to sharpen your focus.

1. **Establishing artificial time constraints**: Allow the person being targeted to feel that there is an end in sight.
2. **Accommodating nonverbals**: Ensure that both your body language as well as your voice is non-threatening.
3. **Slower rate of speech**: Don't oversell and talk too fast. You lose credibility quickly and come on too strong and threatening.
4. **Sympathy or assistance theme**: Human beings are genetically coded to provide assistance and help. It also appeals to their ego that they may know more than you.
5. **Ego suspension**: Most likely the hardest technique but without a doubt the most effective. Don't build yourself up, build someone else up and you will have strong rapport.
6. **Validate others**: Human beings crave being connected and accepted. Validation feeds this need and few give it. Be the great validator and have instant, great rapport.
7. **Ask... How? When? Why? :** When you want to dig deep and make a connection, there is no better or

safer way than asking these questions. They will tell you what they are willing to talk about.

8. **Connect with quid pro quo**: Some people are just more guarded than others. Allow them to feel comfortable by giving a little about you. Don't overdo it.

9. **Gift giving (reciprocal altruism)**: Human beings are genetically coded to reciprocate gifts given. Give a gift, either intangible or material, and seek a conversation and rapport in return.

10. **Managing expectations**: Avoid both disappointment as well as the look of a bad salesman by ensuring that your methods are focused on benefitting the targeted individual and not you. Ultimately you will win, but your mindset needs to focus on them.

You now have the top ten secrets on how to build rapport with anyone in just a few minutes. There is nothing in these pages that each of us has not already done or continues to do every day of our lives; but, when you put conscious thought and planning into every engagement, the consistent results will be tremendous. I continually am amazed at how effective these techniques are in every aspect of my life. I use them with my wife, children, friends, neighbors, coworkers, and spies. These techniques are tried and true and will benefit you in immeasurable ways.

Before I use these techniques or send any class out to practice these techniques, I remind myself and them of on everlasting rule that will dramatically increase your probabilit of success; it is all about them. The only goal I have either fo myself or the individuals I teach is that in every interaction th other person should walk away feeling much better for having met you. You should brighten their day and listen to them when no one else will. Build that connection where others wouldn't and you will have mastered both conversations and quick rapport.

The best and most effective way to get better and more fluid with these techniques is to continually practice them. I have included some exercises in the next section. These exercises are simple and don't take much time. They will help you to practice the techniques and more importantly, how to adapt them to your own personality. These skills must be kept sharp with everyday practice.

I would be remiss if I did not highlight this warning once more. Once you have rapport then compliance with requests is easy. **Warning - the content in this book is so effective that I warn the reader to think carefully how it is used. I do not endorse or condone the use of these skills in malicious or deceptive ways ** Go forth, enjoy your new skills and "enter the Arena!" Make the world a better place.

Practice Exercises:

Each exercise is meant to build upon the last. The effec of each of them used together will add to your confidence as wel as success with building rapport rapidly.

One of the most important aspects to keep in minc throughout your practice is maintaining accommodating nonverbal behavior. Refer back to "Technique 2" if needed anc practice a few of the techniques described.

I have a few good friends and family members that builc tremendous rapport and induce strangers to initiate conversation with them, based upon nonverbal behavior alone. Lookin; nonthreatening and accommodating will be a natural magnet t individuals seeking comfort and validation. When you maste accommodating nonverbals, all the other techniques will flov more easily.

Step 1: Make your opening statement with your bod bladed away as if you were about to walk away.

Step 2: Speak slightly over your shoulder, keep yot chin angle a bit lower and have a genuine smile. The type c smile you would have if someone just did you a favor. Th reality of this situation is that someone is about to do you favor. Your positive nonthreatening nonverbals will induce th favor.

Exercise 1: Third Party Reference

Challenging: I suggest a technique I like to call the "third party reference." A third party reference conversation is one where you have sought an opinion about something other than yourself or the individual you are chatting with. When you ask an opinion about a book in a book store, an item on a shelf in a food store or a headline in the newspaper while waiting to check out, you will be chatting about non-threatening neutral topics. The challenge is identifying one and planning on how to keep a conversation going once initiated.

Step 1: Ensure you are utilizing accommodating nonverbals.

Step 2: Identify an individual and your third party reference.

Step 3: When you have identified both the individual and the third party reference, ask the individual's thought or opinion of the third party reference.

For example, while in a food store you can be looking in the chips aisle. When another individual is also looking in the section you can simply state, "I'm sorry to bother you but I am on my way out, I'm looking to get something for my _____." I like to add "my wife" in the blank. By adding my wife I don't look as though I am trying to "pick them up."

The exercise is simple and straight forward. It will begin to build the muscle memory needed to continue on with the other techniques.

Advanced: This exercise is a bit more complex and very similar to one of my stories at the beginning of the book.

Step 1: Ensure you are utilizing accommodating nonverbals.

Step 2: Choose an appropriate theme that fits you, your personality, and something that you will use on other exercises that you can build upon.

For the purpose of keeping the theme natural, non-threatening, as well as a topic that all individuals can relate to I suggest, "The age when children should start working." This topic is very much like the one about dating age in that individuals have an opinion and have experienced it themselves. For myself, I am able to use my children and the age that my wife and I both think is appropriate. If you do not have children you can use a conversation about someone else's children. You can even reference this exercise in this book. No lies, no subterfuge, just a conversation with a plan and purpose.

Step 3: Go out and try it.

I suggest keeping it easy. I like engaging people that just look to be browsing rather than in a rush to get somewhere. I like large public venues such as a local bar and grille, bookstores, coffee houses, and grocery stores. The more casual an individual you select, the greater the engagement potential.

Exercise 2: Artificial Time Constraints

Challenging: This challenging exercise will build directly upon the first. Establishing artificial time constraints, utilizing accommodating nonverbals, and using a third party reference will all take place almost simultaneously. When you utilize an artificial time constraint, the individual you are speaking with will appreciate that the dialogue will be short and he or she will be more willing to converse.

Step 1: Ensure you are utilizing accommodating nonverbals.

Step 2: Identify an individual and your third party reference.

Step 3: When you have identified both the individual and the third party reference, ask the individual's thought or opinion of the third party reference.

Step 4: Establish an artificial time constraint. For example, while in a food store you can be looking in the cookie aisle. When an individual is also looking in the section you can simply state, "I'm sorry to bother you *but I am on my way out*, I'm looking to get something for my _____." "But I am on my way out" is the artificial time constraint.

Step 5: Go out and try it.

Advanced: Try challenging yourself with different types of artificial time constraints.

Step 1: Ensure you are utilizing accommodating nonverbals.

Step 2: Choose an appropriate theme that fits you, your personality, and something that you will use on other exercises that you can build upon.

Step 3: Following your theme selection you next have to go out and try it.

Step 4: Other possible artificial time constraints are:

- I have to go in a minute, my _____ is waiting.

- I'm late for _____, may I ask your opinion about something.

- I have to get back to my _____, may I ask your opinion about something.

Exercise 3: Slower Rate of Speech

Challenging: This challenging exercise will build directly upon the first two exercises by ensuring that you don't sound like you are overselling.

Step 1: Ensure you are utilizing accommodating nonverbals.

Step 2: Choose an appropriate theme that fits you, your personality, and something that you will use on other exercises that you can build upon.

Step 3: Add an artificial time constraint.

Step 4: Add a slower rate of speech. Simply ensure that you are speaking a little slower and making eye contact. By speaking slower you will also be more focused and relaxed about the words that you are saying. When you slow down you also have the ability to listen to the responses better. This added listening benefit will pay dividends in future techniques and exercises.

Step 5: Go out and try it.

Exercise 4: Sympathy or Assistance Theme

Challenging: This challenging exercise will build directly upon the first three exercises by adding a sympathy and assistance theme.

Step 1: Ensure you are utilizing accommodating nonverbals.

Step 2: Choose an appropriate theme that fits you, your personality, and something that you will use on other exercises that you can build upon.

Step 3: Add an artificial time constraint.

Step 4: Add a slower rate of speech.

Step 5: Add a Sympathy or Assistance Theme. During the initial engagement and third party reference question, modify the question to include sympathy or assistance. For example "I'm sorry to bother you but I am on my way out. *I was hoping you could help me.* I'm looking to get something special for my _____.

Step 6: Go out and try it.

A great example of the sympathy or assistance theme in action goes back to some of my earlier examples. When my friend was interested in obtaining a photograph of the knee-high boots from the young lady at the coffee-house counter, I utilized all of the techniques we have discussed so far. I first started by ensuring that I established an artificial time constraint by letting her know verbally I only had a second and had to get back to my friend. When I made my initial statements I checked myself to ensure that I had accommodating nonverbals. I made sure that my chin was angled down, that I had a slight head tilt and smile. I angled my body so that I was talking slightly over my shoulder to her. I knew exactly what I wanted to say, but I made sure I did not say it too quickly. I used a slower rate of speech so as not to seem "threatening" and that she could clearly understand me. When individuals are not initially clear about why you are chatting with them, they may quickly disengage because they may perceive a threat. The next critical technique was carried out when I asked for her help with the fact that my friend was interested in purchasing the same boots for his wife. The young lady was more than happy to assist and help me.

Exercise 5: Ego Suspension

I have found that suspending the ego is probably the single hardest thing an individual can continuously exercise throughout his or her lifetime. It is also the single most effective tool for developing rapport, having great conversations, and developing meaningful relationships. Suspending your ego means that you are putting another's needs, wants, and opinions ahead of yours.

Challenge 1: This exercise differs slightly than the others because it is an infusion of the skill throughout not just your exercises but every minute of your daily life.

Step 1: Approach someone that you already know. A greater challenge would be to approach a stranger.

Step 2: Identify a topic that you and a friend disagree upon. This can range from politics to child rearing, to Apple vs Windows operating systems.

Step 3: Ask what the individual thinks about the topic knowing it is different than yours. Then, do not correct them.

Step 4: Encourage them to elaborate and explain their reasoning. Nod your head and acknowledge that those are interesting points.

Doing these few simple ego suspending tasks will enable people to feel much more comfortable around you because at the very least, it is a non-confrontational dialogue.

Challenge 2: "It's Not All About Me."

This exercise is the easiest to describe but the hardest to conduct.

Step 1: You have to be very patient to wait for a situation where you are challenged on your thoughts or opinions.

Step 2: Let the other person know that they are correct, and not argue with them.

The easiest example I have is my road rage situation described earlier. I thought I was correct, or at least had an explanation for my actions. It is very difficult to suspend your ego and not correct someone.

Step 3: You cannot provide an explanation or justification for your actions. People truly do not care, they just want to hear you admit they were right and you were wrong.

Step 4: Each of our days has a few occasions where this happens. The next time you think you are right, suspend your ego and don't have the need to correct others.

Step 5: Go out and try it.

Exercise Summary:

These five exercises should give you a great opportunity to go out and practice these skills so that you can fit the techniques to your own personality. The more you practice the better you will be. Eventually, you will be treating individuals in your life very well all of the time. People will want to be around you and you will not understand why. They will return the gifts of validation that you have offered in many ways and enrich your life. Ultimately, you will value and be valued at a much deeper level by all the individuals you interact with and build quick rapport and have great conversations.

This exercise pyramid illustrates the building process:

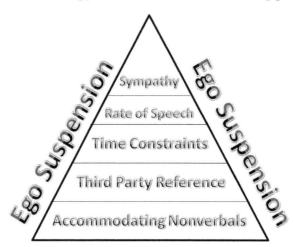

Bibliography

Alessandra, Tony & O'Conner, Michael J. (1994). *People Smarts: Bending the Golden Rule to Give Others What They Want.* San Diego: Pfeiffer & Company.

Alessandra, Tony & O'Conner, Michael J. (1996). *The Platinum Rule: Discover the Four Basic Business Personalities and How They Can Lead You to Success.* New York: Warner Books.

Briggs-Myers, Isabel & Myers, Peter. (1980) *Gifts Differing: Understanding Personality Type.* California: Davies-Black Publishing.

Burnham, Terry & Phelan, Jay. (2000). *Mean Genes: From Sex to Money to Food Taming Our Primal Instincts.* New York: Penguine Books.

Carnegie, Dale. (1990). *How to Win Friends and Influence People.* New York: Pocket Books.

Dreeke, Robin. (2009). It's All About Them: Tools and Techniques for Interviewing and Human Source Development. *FBI Law Enforcement Bulletin*, (June): 1-9.

Dreeke, Robin, Navarro, Joe. (2009). Behavioral Mirroring in Interviewing. *FBI Law Enforcement Bulletin*, (December): 1-10.

Dreeke, Robin, Sidener, Kara. (2010). Proactive Human Source Development. *FBI Law Enforcement Bulletin*, (November): 1-9.

Goldman, Daniel. (1995). *Emotional Intelligence.* New York: Bantam Books.

Gosling, Sam. (2008). *Snoop: What Your Stuff Says About You* New York: Basic Books.

Hadnagy, Christopher. (2011). *Social Engineering: The Art of Human Hacking*. Indianapolis: Wiley Publishing Inc.

Hoffer, Eric. (1989). *The True Believer: Thoughts on the Nature of Mass Movements*. New York: Harpers and Row, Publishers.

Jaye, Aye. (1997). *The Golden Rule of Schmoozing: The Authentic Practice of Treating Others Well*. Naperville, Illinois Sourcebooks.

Keirsey, David & Bates, Marilyn. (1978). *Please Understand Me: Character and Temperament Types.* California: Prometheus Nemsis Book Company.

Kroeger, Otto, & Thuesen, Janet M. (1988). *Type Talk: The 1 Personality Types that Determine How We Live, Love, and Work*. New York: Dell Trade Paperback.

Kushner, Harold S. (2001). *Living a Life that Matters*. New York: Anchor Books.

Kushner, Harold S. (1986). *When All You've Ever Wanted Isn Enough*. New York: Fireside Books.

Kushner, Harold S. (1980). *When Bad Things Happen to Good People*. New York: Avon.

Lowndes, Leil. (2003). *How to Talk to Anyone: 92 Little Tricks for Big Successe in Relationships*. Columbus, Ohio: McGraw Hill.

McClish, Mark. (2001). *I Know You Are Lying*. Winterville, North Carolina: Policeemployment.com.

Morris, Lois B., & Oldham, John M. (1995). *New Personality Self-Portrait: Why You Think, Work, Love, and Act the Way You Do*. New York: Bantam Books.

Napier, Michael R. (2010). *Behavior, Truth and Deception: Applying Profiling and Analysis to the Interview Process*. Boca Raton, Florida: CRC Press.

Navarro. Joe. (2008). *What Every Body is Saying: An Ex-FBI Agent's Guide to Speed-Reading People*. New York: Harper Collins.

Nolan, John. (1996). *Confidential: Business Secrets: Getting Theirs – Keeping Yours*.   Medford Lakes, New Jersey: Yardley Chambers.

Rabon, Don. (2003). *Investigative Discourse Analysis*. Durham, North Carolina: Carolina Academic Press.

Sheehy, Gail. (1977). *Passages: Predictable Crises of Adult Life*. New York: Bantam Books.

The Author

Robin Dreeke is in charge of the Federal Bureau of Investigation's elite Counterintelligence Behavioral Analysis Program (BAP). Although Robin always had aspired to become a great leader, he realized from his time at the United States Naval Academy and in the United States Marine Corps that leadership was much more than just telling people what to do: a great leader uses interpersonal skills to influence, rather than command, others. As a commander in charge of over 200 recruits and 16 drill instructors at Parris Island, South Carolina, Robin learned the fundamentals of leadership and influence. Upon entering service in the FBI in 1997, Robin was assigned to the FBI's New York field office where he was tasked to recruit spies and confidential human sources in the agency's efforts to thwart the effort of our country's adversaries. Along his journey, Robin was accepted as a field assessor for the BAP and received advanced training and experience in the area of social psychology and the practical application of the science behind relationship development.

Robin's remarkable journey began as a 1992 graduate of the United States Naval Academy and former U. S. Marine Corps Officer. He has studied interpersonal relations for the past 23 years of his government service. Through observations of nonverbal behavior, use of the Personal Discernment Inventory, the Myers Briggs Type Indicator, and his own unique techniques, Robin has built highly effective tools for all aspects and stages of interpersonal communication. For over fourteen years, Robin has applied and taught his tools and techniques for the FBI as a member and National Program Manager of the Counterintelligence Division's elite Behavioral Analysis Program. Robin has combined all these tools and techniques and created a one-of-a-kind formula for success with people.

Today, Robin is a recognized expert, author, and gifted lecturer in the art of interpersonal communication. These skills are used every day in leadership, sales, human resources, and all relationships, both business and personal.

For more information, please visit:

http://www.peopleformula.com

CPSIA information can be obtained
at www.ICGtesting.com
Printed in the USA
BVHW04s2224250618
520047BV00012B/65/P